DRESSING UP

How To Find Your
Perfect Personal Style

Scott Smythe

10-10-10
Publishing

Dressing Up
How To Find Your Perfect Personal style
Scott Smythe
www.DressingUpNow.com

Copyright © 2019 by Scott Smythe

Illustrations by Jamison Smythe
Illustrations copyright © Scott Smythe

ISBN: 978-1-77277-297-5

Published by:
10-10-10 Publishing
Markham, Ontario

Contents

Dedication   v
Acknowledgments   vii
Foreword   ix

Chapter 1: The Different Forms Of Style   **1**
How Do You Want the World to See You?   2
The When, Where, and Why of Use   12
What Each Style Says About You   16

Chapter 2: The Style Pyramid   **27**
Nail the Fit   27
Fabric   30
Function   32

Chapter 3: Clothing Item Basics   **37**
The Difference Between Clothes   37
What Can Work Together to Create a Great
Outfit?   40

Chapter 4: Leveraging Colors   **45**
Why Adding Color Is the Key to Looking Great   45
What Colors Work Best and What They Represent   46

Chapter 5: Footwear Basics   **51**
Types of Footwear   51
Formality and Perspectives   54

Chapter 6: Grooming Basics   **63**
Alright, Let's Talk About Hair!   63
Choosing Your Style   65
To Shave or Not to Shave   71

Chapter 7: Accessories   **77**
What Is an Accessory?   77
How They Can Improve Your Look   78

Chapter 8: Quality Over Quantity   **85**
What Counts as Quality?   85
Why It Can Save You Money in the Long Term   87
The Attitude of Wealth   89
There Are Exceptions   90

Chapter 9: Find Your Style   **95**
Everyone's Style Is Unique   95
What Experimenting Involves and
Why You Should Do It   96
Adapting Your Style for Different Events/
Functions, and When to Respect the Guidelines   98

Chapter 10: Have Fun and Be Confident   **105**
Wear the Outfit – Build Confidence by Dressing
Your Style Whenever You Can   105

Recap of Main Points   111
Glossary   119
About the Author   129

This book is dedicated to the handful
of individuals that actually read this through.
May you apply the knowledge gained to create
the world you could only see in your imagination.

Foreword

Have you ever questioned your worth, not entirely sure of who you are and believing that the "Good Life" is only a pipe dream? What you wear has a significant impact on how you view yourself, and how others view you. If you don't feel confident wearing what you currently wear, perhaps it's time to change. Finding a style that fills you with confidence is so important in life. When you are confident, the world around you will seem brighter and full of opportunity. It doesn't matter if you choose more casual clothes or head the more formal route, as long as it fills you with confidence.

In *Dressing Up: How To Find Your Perfect Personal Style,* you will find the necessary information to level up your style. Author Scott Smythe has created a simple, easy to read style guide to make your journey into fashion that much easier. How you dress is how the world will perceive you, and you want to make a good impression. It is one thing to dress well; it is another thing entirely to make a style personal to you, and Scott has laid the path for you to do just that.

Looking good is one of my intentions in life, and what I wear plays a huge part in it. I was delighted to hear that I was not alone in this. It was clear that Scott felt the same way after he had attended some of my courses. In every one, he stood out, dressing up more than most but also understanding what style would be most appropriate for each event.

Scott has the potential to change the world, and he plans to start that process by helping you look great and feel confident. His understanding of style and how it can be used will surely help you along your path to finding *Your Perfect Personal Style*.

Raymond Aaron
New York Times Bestselling Author

Acknowledgments

Antonio Centeno, over at *Real Men Real Style*, for introducing me to style, what it represents, and how it can be used. I was never into style, and rarely, if ever, dressed up. One day, I just happened to find myself watching one of your videos and, suddenly, my mindset was completely changed. I have used the information you have so kindly given to the world, and created something amazing from it. If not for you, this book would not exist. Thank you very much, Antonio.

The Cast of Critical Role. Matthew Mercer, Marisha Ray, Travis Willingham, Laura Bailey, Liam O'Brien, Sam Reigel, Taliesin Jaffe, and Ashley Johnson. Thank you for providing such wonderful entertainment and joy to the world. It feels like waking up on Christmas morning every time a new episode comes out. You have managed to put a smile on my face and the faces of thousands of others, whether it be through your brilliant banter on set or through the many wondrous charities you have supported. Although I'm sure the last place you would expect this would be in a men's style book, I am still a nerd at heart. Thank you again for the entertainment and joy you bring to life. As a wise man once said, "Life needs things to live."

Raymond Aaron. Thank you so much for being my mentor, and a mentor to so many others. You are one of the most generous people I have had the pleasure of meeting. Your knowledge and wisdom is something I cherish and have great respect for. Thanks to you, I was given the opportunity to write this book. As you hold it, know that this is the key that will get me started in the game of life. Thank you for everything, Raymond.

The Smythe Family. Wendy, Dave, and Jamison, thank you all for deviating from the social norm. Wendy and Dave, you decided to walk a path that few have walked. It was always a risk, as is everything in life, but if you had not taken it, our family as a whole would have missed the personal development journey that we all undertake. Thank you for showing me the right path and guiding me along it as you have thus far. There have certainly been ups and downs, with hindsight stalking us closely along the way. But this has yielded some great lessons learned, and we had fun along the way. There was a period when I fell off the wagon and let you all storm ahead. I'm very grateful that you came back to pick me up so we could take this journey together. Jamie, being my brother, I still feel the need on an instinctual level to say that you are a pain in my butt. However, your progress in life has not gone unnoticed, and I am glad that you marched on ahead in your development journey. This gave me a good push to pick up from where I left off and chase you down the path. Being your sibling, I couldn't stand by and watch you win without some competition. So, thank you all for being so awesome and supportive.

The Mulberry Squad. Dave, Wendy, and Jamison Smythe, Eric, Linda and Markus Chan, Kat Nieh, Florence Ng, Aslan Mirkalami, Sergey Poltev, and Raymond Aaron. Thank you all for being part of such a unique and mind blowing weekend. It was a life changing experience for us all, and I couldn't think of a better group of people to do it with. It truly is wonderful to have you all in my life. The knowledge and passion this family has, can and will impact the world. It was a pleasure.

Kat Nieh. It is hard to find people in this world that truly care for others, let alone go out of their way to help them. Kat, I am so grateful for everything you have done for me. You gave me a huge kick up the butt to go and do all of the things I couldn't be bothered to do or was too scared to act on. Somehow you managed to push me out my comfort zones like no other has done before, and for that, I have no words. Cancun broke a lot of boundaries for me, and now I seem eager to do what scares me, more than I ever had before. You keep me accountable for the actions I promised to keep and, because of that, I have never been as productive in my life. Thank you for supporting and encouraging me along the way. I am very grateful to have you in my life and as part of the family.

Chapter 1

The Different Forms of Style

Style forms are outfits made up of certain wardrobe items. There are eight primary forms of style that are generally known: Sloppy/Untidy, Ultra-Casual, Casual, Smart Casual, Business Casual, Business, Black Tie & White Tie.

The vast majority of people seem to wear the casual form of dressing. This is due to several reasons: 1) it's comfortable, 2) it's convenient, 3) it's generally cheap.

There is absolutely nothing wrong with casual dress. It offers the most flexibility of all the style forms, making it an essential part of the hierarchy of style.

The hierarchy of style, as I like to call it, is an all-encompassing format that applies to men, women, and anyone in between. Depending on what an individual may want to achieve, they will choose a style form that suits their needs, whether they are conscious of it or not.

The style you choose will determine how the world views you and how you feel about yourself, and it has the potential to open many more paths in your future. The average human being judges you within 3 seconds of seeing you. Most people are unaware that they are judging you, but regardless, it will leave a lasting impression on them. That is why these few seconds are crucial to building your credibility.

How Do You Want the World to See You?

So, the question now is: How do you want the world to see you? Will you be viewed as a slob who couldn't care about their image, or will you command the room and gain the respect you know you deserve. There are many ways of doing this. I have known many people who have tried to adopt the higher levels of the styles, such as Business/Business Casual and Black tie, with no luck in swaying people's opinions of them. On the other hand, I have also known many people who prefer to dress much more casual, and have had massive success in commanding the room and gaining instant respect from the people around them.

The only way to succeed is actually to use the information you will find in this book.

Now that I have gone over the primary forms of style, you need to know what is involved. So, what is involved?

The Different Forms of Style

Each form of style is made up of particular articles of clothing and clothing combinations. The easiest of the style forms to use for demonstration purposes would be Business. Business is the use of a suit, dress shirt, tie, and dress shoes. The suit is made up of the jacket, pants, and occasionally a vest, and they should all be made of matching material, meaning all parts of the suit have been cut from the same cloth.

Now, let me go over the basics of what each style form is generally made up of.

Sloppy/Untidy

You may have already guessed, but this form uses oversized, dirty, damaged, or inappropriate articles of clothing.

Ultra-Casual

This generally consists of very basic articles of clothing. An example would be someone who knows they don't need to leave the house, and doesn't see the need to wear much. A thin white undershirt and pair of sweatpants will do.

Casual
The most common style form, this form generally consists of a short/long sleeves, jeans or shorts, and shoes.

Smart Casual

This style consists of a well-fitted shirt/dress shirt with collar, and khakis, chinos, or jeans, and a pair of dress shoes/loafers.

Business Casual
This style takes aspects of both Smart Casual and Business styles. This style can consist of a dress shirt, khakis, chinos or jeans, dress shoes/boots, and a sports coat or blazer.

Business

As stated prior, this style should consist of a matching suit, dress shirt, tie, and dress shoes.

Black Tie

This style is generally to be used on special occasions, and consists of a Tuxedo suit, black dress shoes, black bowtie, and a Tuxedo shirt.

White Tie

Without a doubt, the rarest style. White tie is to be used in extremely specific and unique situations. It generally consists of a black tailcoat jacket and matching pants, black dress shoes, a white dress shirt/Tuxedo shirt, white bowtie, white gloves, and a top hat.

The When, Where, and Why of Use

In the next few paragraphs, I will be going over when/where to dress in a particular style, and why it is a good idea to do so. This should give you a good idea of what will be appropriate or what may be inappropriate, depending on the situation.

– Sloppy/Untidy

It is my personal opinion that this form is unacceptable in almost every scenario. I plead you, don't dress this way for any reason.

– Ultra-Casual

Ultra-Casual is acceptable for almost every aspect of your daily routine, as long as you do not enter an area where a higher form of dress is the expectation. Ultra-casual dress would be acceptable if staying home or performing physical activity. Why might it be beneficial to wear Ultra-Casual? A gym, for example, would be a great place where Ultra-Casual would be the expectation. Doing physical activity requires your clothing to be flexible, and it must be able to absorb sweat and odor. Sweatpants and a hoodie are two articles of Ultra-Casual clothing that would be perfect for such a situation. Ultra-Casual clothing would generally be considered the most comfortable of the style forms, having most clothing articles made from a lighter material.

(Ultra-Casual is a form where slightly oversized clothing items may be acceptable.)

– Casual

Casual dress is generally acceptable anywhere. The only occasions it may not be is black tie events or certain business events/meetings. Casual is by far the most common style out there. It is versatile and straightforward, making it ideal for most people. Casual dress should be worn whenever you deem it appropriate. This is because the Casual style has so much functionality and versatility that I cannot tell you accurately when/where it should be worn. That will entirely depend on your situation. The Casual style generally consists of lighter materials and is comfortable to wear.

– Smart Casual

Smart Casual dress is another variant of the Casual style that is meant to represent oneself in a higher manner without having to incorporate articles of clothing such as suits, sports jackets, blazers, ties, etc. This style can be worn anywhere, with exception to black tie events or situations that require increased physical activity.

Wearing the Smart Casual form has many advantages. Being the first style to incorporate smarter articles of clothing, it will help raise people's perspective of you. If done correctly, you will be seen as someone who has their life in order. An appropriate place to wear the Smart Casual style is in an office setting. It would allow you to make a better impression on your employer, and with minimal physical activity, you can style much more. Smart Casual generally consists of layered clothing. Depending on what you wear, this form of dress can be a little heavier than previous styles, and may take some time getting used to.

– Business casual

The Business Casual style is a mix that incorporates aspects of business attire and Smart Casual attire. This style form will present you as someone who understands and influences the business world. This style is much less conservative than the true business dress. It offers a more liberal approach to dressing smart. It can show you to be a more outgoing and creative person, depending on what you use. Business Casual is generally appropriate anywhere other than black tie events. Somewhere it may not be so appropriate would be at meetings where Business dress is needed, or in the unfortunate event of funerals. It is important to note that this style generally incorporates heavier fabrics and articles of clothing, such as sports coats and blazers. That is why it is essential to keep temperature in mind. This style can get uncomfortable in hotter climates if you are not used to it.

– Business

The Business style is the most conservative of the style forms. This style is the first to incorporate a suit. A suit being a jacket and pants made from the same material. The Business style will present you as more conservative and as someone with a good grip on their finances. This style is ideal for corporate environments, meetings, and conferences. There are not many places where it would be unacceptable to wear this style; the only thing to keep in mind is how it might affect your brand, depending on where you are. The Business style uses heavier material and fabric, making it much hotter and more uncomfortable in certain situations. If you live in a warmer climate, I would not recommend wearing this style during the day.

– Black Tie

Black Tie is the most luxurious style form, in my opinion. It is rarely used, as it is meant to be for specific events only. Black Tie is unique because it is conservative in its design and liberal in its presentation. This style is only acceptable at black-tie events. A gala or wedding would be the events Black Tie can and should be worn. Black Tie is not usually acceptable outside of black-tie specific events. It would be considered far too fancy for any other use. This style uses heavier material and fabric, which can make it uncomfortable in hotter climates. Black Tie is generally to be used indoors, and outside only if the event calls for it.

– White Tie

White Tie is by far the rarest style form out there. It is so rare in fact that I have never seen anyone wearing this style. This style is very similar to Black Tie but incorporates much more, such as gloves, top hats, and canes. White Tie should only be used at white-tie events. It is unacceptable to wear White Tie outside of these events. If you were to wear this style elsewhere, instead of raising people's perception of you, it would most likely lower their perception of you. Wearing an outfit like this anywhere other than white-tie events will present you as a fool or as someone trying too hard to stand out. This style uses heavier material and fabric. Because this style has more intricate pieces, it will likely be uncomfortable to most people.

What Each Style Says About You

As you know by now, there are eight main forms of style.

Each form has its benefits and shortcomings in every situation; one of those situations being how others view you. It is very important to understand how you will generally be viewed by others, depending on the style you choose. I inserted a few examples in the previous section so you can get an idea of how it works. Let me go into a bit more detail and use scenarios you would find in the real world.

– Perception of Sloppy

Let me be brutally honest. If you wear sloppy or untidy clothing, whether it be by choice or not, the amount of respect you will get from people will drop drastically. Wearing sloppy clothing designates you as someone who is unorganized, messy, and potentially untrustworthy. If you have a go-for-it life attitude, and you are generally a very happy person, you will still find that people will think less of you just from your dress. Remember, it takes only three seconds for someone to make an opinion of you just by looking. If they don't see your cheerful attitude within those three seconds, chances are they will put you down in their estimation. The effect of this is even more prominent if you happen to be someone with a negative view on life.

– Perception of Ultra-Casual

Wearing Ultra-Casual clothing is mostly used for physical exercise or as a temporary dress if you have nowhere to go. The Ultra-Casual dress will generally designate you as someone who is either physically active, constantly in a rush, or just lazy and would prefer to spend the day lying in bed. Why do I say that these will be designated to you? Well, let me provide a few examples. As I mentioned in the previous pages, Ultra-Casual is a very good dress for physical activity. It is generally loose and allows for extra motion, the absorption of sweat, or the flow of air— perfect for gym clothing.

On the other hand, Ultra-Casual will likely be the first clothes you put on if you need to rush out somewhere. For example, if you had a dentist appointment, and you slept in too late and needed clothes that you could quickly slip on. Lastly, is the example of laziness. Ultra-Casual clothing is the perfect dress for just staying at home if you don't have to go anywhere. That being said, it can grow to be a part of your brand if that is all you wear. You might choose to continue wearing ultra casual even if you do head out.

– Perception of Casual

The Casual dress style is the style that will likely have the least effect on how people perceive you. Casual dress is the most common, so for most people, they will think nothing of it. They will, of course, still judge more positively or negatively depending on how you arrange your clothes, but it will not have as much impact as it would with any other style. If you choose to wear Casual dress, you will blend into a crowd, and people will likely forget about you. They will see you as just average, and that's not what you want.

– Perception of Smart Casual

Smart Casual dress is where you will likely start noticing more positive reactions to how you dress. Smart Casual will put you a step above anyone wearing Casual, and people will certainly notice. If someone sees you wearing Smart Casual clothing, they will generally perceive you to be organized, intelligent, and stable. Why might you be perceived this way? To dress in the Smart Casual style requires an organized environment to easily find the right articles of clothing. It requires a certain degree of skill to make sure the clothes match and complement each other's features. Lastly, if you have the time to go through the effort of making sure your outfit works well and looks good, you probably take the time to look after yourself.

– Perception of Business Casual

Business Casual is where you will notice even more reactions toward you. This style is unique because it has the potential for people to perceive you as having both a conservative and liberal balance to life. Business Casual is, as it says, more casual. It also brings a bit of creativity to your dress and personality. You will generally be perceived as being more creative, outgoing, and happy, but also organized and intelligent.

This is because of how the style is set up. It combines aspects of Smart Casual, which gives the perception of intellect and organization—the Business aspects that lean more toward conservative and being to the point. What generally makes a Business Casual style is the incorporation of a blazer or sports jacket. These are what lends to the more liberal, creative, and outgoing perceptions of the style. A sports coat certainly adds a feeling of playfulness to your presentation. People will most likely enjoy your company and time.

– Perception of Business

The Business style has the most conservative feel and look of all the style forms. With this, comes a different perception from others. While wearing Business dress, you will likely be perceived to be more conservative, organized, to the point, and important. The reasons for these are as follows. People will see you as being more conservative because of the way suits were used and how they are portrayed in the media. Suits were items only the wealthy could afford. That was generally due to the more conservative business acumen of said individuals who kept the money for themselves. Media has also similarly portrayed suits (in this light). Both are generally using the idea of greed. Going along with the conservative persona, you will be viewed as a no-nonsense, straight-to-the-point individual. This also is the case when you think again of the general view on conservative businessmen. You will also be seen as a more organized person; this is because it takes effort and planning to put together a suit that looks great and that you would wear often. There is a very good chance that you will be treated with more respect due to how you are viewed as an important individual. People may not know the reason, but they will deem you to be more important because of the social hierarchy. Someone wearing a suit has, throughout history, been viewed as higher on the social scale.

– Perception of Black Tie

Black Tie is another unique style that incorporates conservative and liberal aspects. Generally, people's perceptions of someone in Black Tie depends on where they are. As I previously stated, if you were to wear Black Tie outside of a black-tie event, people's perceptions of you may be lowered because it would not be appropriate or normal to do so. However, in most circumstances, people will view you as being outgoing, organized, and exciting. People will assume that you are outgoing and organized because of what the suit represents: It is to be used at events that generally involve some kind of party or dance, and it takes time and effort to put together a tuxedo that is neat and tidy. Lastly, they will think you're exciting. This also plays from the fact that you would be attending fun events, but also from the fact that the suit itself gives a playful vibe.

– Perception of White Tie

There is not much to talk about regarding the perception of White Tie. If you are at an event that allows or requires White Tie, you will be seen as accommodating, fun, tidy/organized, and agree-able. The reasons for this had been stated earlier. If you are wearing White Tie outside of an appropriate event, people's perceptions of you will be lowered dramatically, as they will see you as a comedian.

Look at Some Examples

The best way for you to get an idea of what style might suit you best is to look at some examples. It seems pretty simple, but that's the best solution. Look at a whole selection of outfits and determine what would work best for you. You could go online and look through some pictures of models wearing certain style forms. Learning by example is the best way to get started. Once you understand this, and master the basics, you can create your unique style.

Truth be told, there are many different style forms out there, each taking inspiration from one or more of the eight main forms. Your task before moving onto the next chapter is to find some examples of dress that you think would be best for you. When you do, write down what aspects of the outfit you like or find useful. What I would recommend you do is to print off the images you like, and pin them to a board. This way, you can outline all the options in order to see them clearly. Once you have done this, we can delve back into detail of what makes them look so perfect.

You can find full size, color, print-ready examples on my website, at www.DressingUpNow.com

"People will stare.
Make it worth their while."
– Harry Winston

After every chapter, there will be a few pages of notes. I have added these to give you a quick and easy way to write down any ideas you may have floating around in your head. Any outfit combinations you can think of, or any ways you could use this information to improve your wardrobe, are just a few possible uses for the notes section.

Notes

_____

_____

_____

_____

_____

_____

_____

_____

_____

_____

_____

_____

_____

Notes

_____

_____

_____

_____

_____

_____

_____

_____

_____

_____

_____

_____

_____

Chapter 2

The Style Pyramid

Nail the Fit

Oh, the fit. I would have to argue that fit is the most important aspect of dressing well. Fit is the most important part of what is called the *Style Pyramid*, which is a representation of the three most important aspects of clothing: The *fit* of the clothes, the *fabric* of the clothes, and the *function* of the clothes. The fit is what truly brings an outfit together. You could have the most beautiful, elegant suit that is worth a small fortune, but if it doesn't fit you, then it is essentially worthless to you. You do not want to wear a suit that does not fit. So, why is fit so important? To get an article of clothing fitted to your body instantly makes it unique and personal. You will be the only person in the world to have clothing that fits your body perfectly. Anyone could try on your clothing, but it would never be perfect.

Having clothing that fits correctly makes you look more tidy and presentable. Even if your chosen style is Casual, getting your clothes fitted makes such an impact on how tidy you look and how tall you look, and it can make you look thinner if you happen to be a larger build. Now, I must say that other aspects of your clothing can affect this in many ways, but *fit* will always be top.

If you would like a visual representation to help better your understanding of what I just mentioned, here is an image that represents the difference between just wearing a suit and wearing one that fits correctly.

If you would like to see this image in more detail, as well as any other images within this book, please visit DressingUpNow.com

There are a few ways to get your clothing to fit you correctly.

Getting custom made clothing is the best way to have clothes that fit you perfectly. You can do this through certain online retailers or in person by a skilled tailor. If you choose this method to get your clothes fitted correctly, it will likely produce the best results, but it will also be quite expensive. If finance is something you need to track, I would recommend the second option: finding a tailor.

Bringing clothes you already own to a skilled tailor is the method I would recommend for anyone starting their journey in personal style. A good tailor can make almost any article of clothing fit perfectly. There is some size limitation, depending on what you want tailored. A good tailor will tell you what they can work with and what they can't, and if the article of clothing you bought can be adjusted. Getting your clothes tailored allows you to get well-fitted clothing without breaking the bank.

The last option is to tailor your clothing personally. This is something I only recommend to those who have the skill set and equipment to do it. Even then, I highly recommend only working on small adjustments, such as the hem of a pair of pants. You don't want to risk damaging your clothing.

Fabric

What is the point of the fabric? As I mentioned above, the fabric is part of the style pyramid. Fabric is the material and weave of your clothing, which means it plays a huge part in how your clothing will work for you and complement your overall outfit.

Let's start with the basics of fabric in relation to clothing. The majority of clothing on the market is made of cotton. Cotton is widely used, thanks to its soft touch, durability, flexibility, adaptability, and cost. Next, there is the weave of the clothing. The weave is how the cotton was intertwined together to create a larger, more solid material. There are many different types of weaves you will find in clothing. The most common ones you will find will be the plain weave, oxford weave, twill weave, and herringbone weave.

Why does this matter? The material and weave of your clothing will affect many aspects of your new wardrobe. It can be as simple as how comfortable it makes you feel, to the more complicated matters of matching your clothing so that everything is complementary. Cotton is the material you will be working with, regardless of the style form you choose to emulate. Being a soft fabric, you should generally feel comfortable wearing it; however, this is where the weave can become a large factor. Most casual clothing will use a plain weave, as it is the most simple of the weaves and easiest to produce. If you are looking to take inspiration from a more formal style, an oxford or twill weave is what you will see in most dress shirts.

This is important because each weave has its own unique property. I'm sure you have heard of breathable clothing. The breathability of the clothing is factored in by the material used, its thickness, and the weave. Tighter weaves, such as twill weaves, tend to be less breathable.

It is important that you understand the materials and weaves of the clothing you use, so that you can better implement them into your daily routines. Are you someone who gets hot often? Wear a shirt of plain or oxford weave. On the other hand, if you find yourself getting cold, wearing a twill or flannel weave shirt may help.

– Material and Weave in Relation to Formality

It should be of no surprise, but the material and weave of clothing can drastically affect how formal you may appear. Wool is a perfect example of a material that is much more casual looking. Wool is thick and coarse, which makes it less sleek and form-fitting. The weave used in this article of clothing doesn't come into a factor, simply because of the thickness of the material. The same principle can be applied to a dress shirt. A dress shirt on its own is considered more formal, but if it was made using a flannel weave, it becomes more casual.

This is something I believe you won't need to worry about too much as a beginner, as most people are unlikely to notice the smaller details such as the weave. However, if you find yourself surpassing the more basic aspects of dressing up, then I would highly recommend looking more into the materials and weaves of your clothing, and how they will affect your image.

Function

The *function* of your clothing is a huge factor in whether or not you should wear it. There are so many factors to take into account when you put an outfit together. Will this keep me warm? Will it cool me off? Will this be durable enough for my purposes? These are just some questions you may ask yourself, and they give you a good understanding of why the function of your clothing is so important.

As I briefly went over in the last few pages, the material of the clothing is hugely important to its functionality. If you require the function of the clothing to keep you warm, choose a warmer/thicker material, such as wool, or something that uses a flannel weave. If you need to be able to carry many small items, find clothes that have functional pockets. It's not hard to see what I'm getting at. When putting together an outfit, make sure to understand how to include function appropriately. I'll give you an example.

You are going to another conference. Having been to several before, you know that the rooms are cooled, so no one overheats. Of course, it's always a little too cold for your liking, so you decide to bring a long-sleeve sweater to keep you warm. You remember that the conference room doesn't allow larger carrying cases, such as bags or briefcases, to enter, even though you are constantly given small trinkets throughout the event. The long-sleeve sweater you chose does not have any pockets, so you instead switch it out for a blazer, which you know has a few pockets available.

With that all figured out, you can head to the conference knowing that you won't have to worry about these little inconveniences—a quick and very simple example of how the function of your clothing may come into effect.

I feel it necessary to explain how and why the fabric and functional aspects of the style pyramid are where they are. My personal opinion is that the location of these within the pyramid can be switched around as much as you want, as they are so deeply intertwined with each other. The majority of the functions that an article of clothing can provide depends on the material it's made out of. The same can be said in reverse: The materials of the clothing rely upon the function you intend for it. So don't worry about which one is more important than the other. Just understand that *fit* is at the top of the pyramid, and underneath it is *fabric* and *function*, in no discernible order.

"Style is something each of us already has; all we need to do is find it." –
Diane von Furstenberg

Notes

_____

_____

_____

_____

_____

_____

_____

_____

_____

_____

_____

_____

_____

Notes

_____

_____

_____

_____

_____

_____

_____

_____

_____

_____

_____

_____

Chapter 3

Clothing Item Basics

The Difference Between Clothes

The first step you need to take in order to dress with confidence, and to know that you are rocking your perfect personal style, is... to put some clothes on. By all means, if you want to rock the birthday suit, you're more than welcome to; however, I would recommend you do that within the confines of your home. If you need to head out, please do put something on. The question is, what? What should you wear that will help elevate your style to one that you feel confident wearing. The three main articles of clothing you will be wearing, on a day-to- day basis, will be pants, shirts, and jackets, of some description. Notice how I have left out socks and underwear. This is because those items will be much less visible and have less of an effect when it comes to looking your best. That doesn't mean they provide nothing at all (more on that later). However, pants, shirts, and jackets will generally be the most important items within your wardrobe.

There are many different types of pants, shirts, and jackets out there to choose from. Which ones will work best with your style? I am not going to list every type and compare them to one another, because that would be an entire book on its own.

I will make a quick comparison of one particular item to another, then state which style category I believe it will be most effective in.

Let's start with pants. The two I will be comparing are *jeans* and *khakis*.

Jeans are made out of denim, a hardy fabric made of cotton, woven in a tight twill weave, which makes it thicker than other pants using another weave. Jeans come in many colors and have a few variations in design, making them great all-around pants.

Khakis, on the other hand, are made out of cotton, wool, synthetics, and a combination of materials, depending on their intended purpose. For the most part, khakis will be made of cotton, using a serge or plain weave. They are not hardy like jeans, so avoid wearing them when working with heavy equipment. They are much more formal than jeans, and can keep you cooler in hotter climates.

Both have their pros and cons, and those will depend on how you choose to use them. I would classify jeans as part of the Casual style, but they can also work well in Smart Casual, and even Business Casual in some circumstances. Khakis would be part of Smart Casual and Business Casual styles.

Moving onto shirts, let's keep things simple and compare a short-sleeve shirt and a dress shirt.

The short-sleeve shirt is generally made of cotton, woven in a plain weave. They range in thicknesses but generally are more on the thinner side and are not very hardy. Short sleeves are great if you want to keep cool, but they lack if you're looking to keep warm.

Dress shirts are generally made from cotton, in a twill, oxford, or poplin weave. They are thicker than an average short-sleeve shirt, and can be a bit hardy depending on the weave and thickness. Dress shirts are very versatile, making them great all-around shirts. Roll up the sleeves and undo a button to cool off, or button up and roll the sleeves down to keep warm.

It is very obvious, but short-sleeve shirts are part of the Ultra Casual and Casual style forms, while dress shirts range from Smart Casual to White Tie styles.

Lastly, let's compare jackets.

A crewneck sweater will be used, as in this section, I consider a jacket as anything that goes over a shirt. A crew neck sweater will generally be made from wool or cotton. It will be fairly thick and is perfect for keeping you warm, making it a good all-around item.

A blazer will generally be made of cotton, synthetic, or a mix. It is thick, but I would not consider it hardy. It is good for keeping you cool or for warming you up, because of its design. It's made of a thicker material but will not button up all the way.

In conclusion, a crewneck sweater would be part of the Casual and Smart Casual style forms. A blazer would be part of the Business Casual style.

What Can Work Together to Create a Great Outfit?

With the comparisons in mind, let's put together a good looking outfit.

The first step is to determine what style best suits you or what style you would like to try out. Once you have a style you want to take inspiration from, then you need to find the appropriate clothing. My examples of what each style form is generally made from, in Chapter one, will help you choose the right clothing. Let's stick with a more simple and easier to wear style on a day-to-day basis. Smart Casual is the form you choose. By looking at the Smart Casual section in Chapter one, we can see that Smart Casual is generally made up of a well-fitted shirt/dress shirt, and khakis, chinos, or jeans, and a pair of dress shoes/loafers.

What you put together will be affected by the environment you're in. If you live in a hot climate for the majority of the year, you will need to adjust what goes into the outfit. I would recommend, once you have everything you need, to put together the outfit and lay it out in front of you so you can get an idea of what it looks like. You lay out a pair of black jeans, a pair of long, black socks, a pair of black chukka boots, a grey dress shirt, and a black, v-neck sweater. It looks good laid out; you have everything you need. After spending a few minutes putting it all on, you stand in front of a mirror to see how your outfit looks. It looks quite good for your first attempt, and you feel quite confident. However, the more you look, the more you realize something isn't quite right.

You grab a white dress shirt, a dark grey pair of jeans, a brown pair of dress boots, and a brown belt. Putting the outfit back together, you are much happier with the results. You look much better than before.

What made it this way? Why did you have the feeling that something was missing the first time, and what made the big difference once you put the outfit together again? You unknowingly leveraged the power of color. This leads us nicely into the next chapter.

"Anyone can get dressed up and glamorous, but it is how people dress in their days off that are the most intriguing."
– Alexander Wang

Notes

_____

_____

_____

_____

_____

_____

_____

_____

_____

_____

_____

_____

_____

_____

Notes

_____

_____

_____

_____

_____

_____

_____

_____

_____

_____

_____

_____

_____

Chapter 4

Leveraging Colors

Why Adding Color Is the Key to Looking Great

Gentlemen, it's time to talk about *colors*. More specifically, how to leverage them to create an outfit that looks great, makes others notice you, and makes you feel like a king. Color adds so much to an outfit. It makes it so much easier to change the style form you wish to emulate, to take aspects of one form and blend it with another. It can drastically change people's perceptions of you, and can give them an idea of who you are before you even start to speak.

Adding color can make you stand out from the crowd, and when you stand out from the crowd, more opportunities are likely to find their way to you. So, what colors should you bring into your outfits? Well, this all depends on what outfit you are wearing/wish to wear, and what kind of message you want to send out. Let us examine a simple one to start with: a traditional black business suit. If we assume that whoever is wearing it has decided to dress in the true Business style, then his outfit would have a tie. The color of the tie is very important because it will be the first and perhaps the only part of the outfit that uses a differing color. If he decides to use a red tie, it will provide a stark contrast with the rest of his outfit, and it will immediately draw the attention of others.

What Colors Work Best and What They Represent

If you had someone in a suit walk up to you, and they were wearing a red tie, what do you think would likely happen? You would have a glance at his outfit as a whole, and then your eyes would narrow in on his tie. So, just like that, he has your attention, and you know it. The color red also represents much more than simple attention-grabbing. Every color out in the world has a series of emotions that encompass it. Red represents passion; it represents power, and it can represent aggressiveness. That's why I said that the color you choose to wear allows people to understand who you are or how you may act. They inherently know which emotions are represented by certain colors. So this man who is wearing a black business suit and red tie will not only stand out and be noticed, he will likely command the room, as he will be viewed with an aura of passion and leadership.

Now, if this man were to wear a blue tie, things would be different. Depending on how much of a contrast the blue is to the rest of the outfit, he too will stand out. However, he will likely not be viewed as a leader but rather as a calm, collected, and creative individual, as those are some of the emotions that blue represents.

Now, for another example, let us use someone who has decided to dress a bit more casual. They wear simple navy jeans, black shoes, a white dress shirt, and a medium brown sports jacket. This would likely fit into the Business Casual form of dress. What would be the most prominent part of the outfit—that which draws your attention? It would be the brown sports jacket. He could have easily worn a darker colored jacket, but he decided to wear brown. First thing, we notice him. He stands out and has our attention. We see that he looks quite sharp, thanks to this jacket complimenting the rest of his attire. The color brown is a much more earthy color, and generally represents reliability and steadfastness. We might find ourselves trusting him more and having the idea that "this is someone who would stand up for me"—all due to the colors he wore.

Now you should have a good idea of why colors are such a vital part of one's wardrobe. They will help you stand out from the crowd. They will show others who you are, or whom you want them to think you are, and they can hugely compliment your overall outfit, if done correctly. Just remember, experiment with different colors, and see what you like. Once you have found what works for you, go out into the world and command attention.

*"We must never confuse elegance
with snobbery."*
– Yves Saint Laurent

Notes

_____

_____

_____

_____

_____

_____

_____

_____

_____

_____

_____

_____

_____

_____

Notes

_____

_____

_____

_____

_____

_____

_____

_____

_____

_____

_____

_____

_____

_____

Chapter 5

Footwear Basics

Gentlemen, let's talk about what goes on your feet. Footwear can and will improve your outfit immensely if you know how to implement it. Doing so incorrectly will harm your overall outfit. What you wear on your feet can make or break an outfit; so, in this chapter, let me give you a basic overview of the most common types of footwear you will find, the benefits of each type, and what they may say about you, and finally, where they would place on the formality meter.

Types of Footwear

The most common types of footwear can be separated into casual shoes, dress shoes, and boots.

Casual shoes: These are the ones that are likely the most familiar footwear to the largest amount of people. Casual shoes are convenient for everyday living, and are generally cheaper and much more comfortable when compared to dress shoes and boots. The most common casual shoes consist of sneakers, runners, sandals, boat shoes, and slip-ons.

These shoes are not limited to their specific type, meaning that there are shoes that incorporate designs from the ones just mentioned. For example, you may find a slip-on pair of sneakers. It is common to have aspects of different shoes mixed. Not only limited to casual shoes, but most forms of footwear, in general, can be a mix between different types.

Sneakers: Generally rubber-soled softer shoes that are used in recreational sports and general day-to-day activities.

Runners: Lightweight shoes designed to absorb one's body weight to reduce the physical strain during the act of running.

Sandals: Generally lightweight, open-toed, and made from leather or faux leather, with straps that go over the bridge of the foot.

Boat Shoes: Leather or canvas shoes with a rubber sole to provide excellent traction while working on the decks of boats.

Slip-ons: Designed to be put on with ease and that require no lacing for fastening.

Dress Shoes: The shoes everyone first thinks of when there is an opportunity to dress up. They are the most traditional and classic form of footwear when it comes to dressing smart. They are often simple and elegant, and they work with nearly every outfit.

The most common types of dress shoes are *oxfords, derbies, brogues, monk straps,* and *loafers.*

Oxfords: Made from leather, generally have a leather sole, and incorporate a closed lacing system.

Derbies: Very similar to an oxford; in many cases, almost identical. What makes the difference is that a derby uses an open lacing system, compared to an oxford having a closed lacing system.

Brogues: Made from leather, generally have a leather sole, and have a perforation on a wingtip toe (meaning the cap to the shoe is cut into a W shape and has decorative holes punched into it).

Monk Strap: Made of leather, with a leather sole, and uses no lacing system. Instead, it is closed using a buckle.

Loafers: Considered to be the most casual of the dress shoe types. They are generally made of leather and have either a very small heel or no heel at all. These are one of the examples of slip-on shoes.

Boots: My favorite and preferred form of footwear, although I do also use casual and dress shoes. They can be dressed up or down with ease because they are essentially taller dress shoes and are very versatile and durable. The most common boots that can easily be dressed up are chukka boots, chelsea boots, jodhpur boots, and simple lace-up boots.

Chukka: Ankle high boots made from leather or suede. These boots are more distinguishable thanks to the reduced amount of eyelets, which usually only consist of two or three sets.

Chelsea: A unique boot as it does not incorporate the use of lacing at all. Instead, this boot uses elasticized rubber on the sides to allow easy insertion and remove of your foot. Chelsea boots are most commonly made of leather or suede, and use a rubber sole.

Jodhpur: Quite similar to the chelsea boot as it, too, has no lacing system. It is designed to have the vamp pull away to allow one's foot to insert easily. The jodhpur uses a buckle and strap to close the boot securely. It is made from leather and generally uses a rubber sole.

Lace-up: Probably the most common type of boot. They are made of leather, often with few or no designs, and use a rubber sole. Lace-up boots generally go above the ankle and have multiple eyelet sets.

Formality and Perspectives

Now it should be no surprise that each one of the categories of footwear I listed has their general position on the formality meter. I could potentially rank their formality, using the different style forms, but it would require a much more detailed breakdown of the forms, which I do not intend to include in this book. This is a book on the basics, so I'm going to do my best to keep it that way. So, we can't use the style forms— what can we use? Well, it's very simple: a simple line, with *very formal* on one end, and *very casual* on the other.

Formal   Casual

(You can find this image, in full color and print-ready, on my site, DressingUpNow.com.)

As you can see, there are a few points along this meter, depicting different levels of formality. Now that you have an idea of what it looks like, let me give you the generalized location of each class of footwear.

Two of the classes will be very easy to associate their place on the list, because their general formality has already been named. Casual shoes—you guessed it—are going to be lower on the meter, in the casual end of the spectrum. Dress shoes will be in the higher end of the meter, around the formal end of the spectrum. That leaves us with boots. Where would these rank on the meter? Using the boots that I listed previously, I would have to put boots near the middle of the meter, leaning more toward slightly more formal than casual. Although boots are inherently more casual than traditional dress shoes, the type of boot and the designs are generally going to be more formal. This makes boots very good for most situations, as they can easily be dressed up or down.

Now, that will help you get a sense of where your footwear may generally lie on the formality meter. There is one more very important detail: the color of the shoe/boot. Depending on the color, the shoes and boots can be pushed more in one direction on the meter. Boots and shoes come in many colors, and each color has its general place on the formality meter. For example, black is considered more formal than brown. That is a nice and easy example to use because it gets the message across very easily. However, as I said, it's not all black and brown. Oxblood is a color you may often see primarily in dress shoes, and even this has its place and will affect the formality of the shoe. An oxblood shoe will still be very formal, more so than a brown shoe, but less formal than a black one. The same can be said with any piece of footwear. A black boot is more formal than one that is of a different color.

It is quite simple to figure out, as long as you don't jump right into the deep end and start to overanalyze every detail. It will help you determine what you may want to wear, depending on the scenario.

I ask that you take a few minutes to do some work regarding this. Head over to my website, find the Formality meter, and rank where you think your current shoes or boots may lie on it. Do this, and it will give you a great perspective on what your footwear says about you.

Talking about what your shoes say about you; your shoes, much like the clothes you choose to wear, can tell others who you are as an individual. The impact of this is not as profound as the impact your clothes will have on others' perceptions of you, but they do still play a significant part.

A man walks up to you, wearing a perfectly tailored suit, and he is gleaming with confidence. You look him up and down, and he looks amazing. This man must have his life together and must be successful. Then you look down to what he is wearing on his feet, and it's a much different story. He is wearing a pair of sneakers. Now, what will come into your head when you spot that? *It must have slipped his mind, or he had nothing else to wear, or he is a relaxed, fun individual.*

The first two options are very unlikely. He must have known that he was wearing them, as he put them on. If these were the only shoes he could use, his spark of confidence would likely be diminished. So, he is most likely a fun and relaxed guy. However, I do not recommend wearing sneakers with a suit!

That is just one short example to help you understand how someone's footwear can represent who they are. Now, if you were to wear a pair of boots, it would give the vibe that you do like to look good but also want to be prepared for anything. Boots are versatile and can hold up better in adverse conditions. That could be one of the reasons why someone would assume that you like to be prepared.

People's assumptions of you, based on your choice of footwear, is always happening, and most of the time, it is subconsciously. It is unlikely that someone will see your shoes and enter the *thinking-man pose* to determine what kind of person you are. It is possible but unlikely. As I stated earlier in the book, people, on average, judge someone's character within 3 seconds. The shoes you choose on a day-to-day basis will be included as part of the subconscious judgment of character, which is done by everyone you meet.

Let's say you choose to wear classic oxfords. First impressions will offer thoughts of elegance, importance, simplicity, and wealth. Has the idea set in that each type of shoe or boot you wear represents an inherent character trait? Use this information to leverage how you wish to represent yourself. You will generally lean toward the shoe that represents how you view yourself first. In other words, you will choose what represents you on a habitual level, and if you need to dress up for a social occasion, you will be able to choose what you think would represent you better, on a more social level.

With all this information in mind, you will be confident in choosing the right footwear for you.

"I firmly believe that with the right footwear, one can rule the world."
— **Bette Midler**

Notes

_____

_____

_____

_____

_____

_____

_____

_____

_____

_____

_____

_____

_____

Notes

_____

_____

_____

_____

_____

_____

_____

_____

_____

_____

_____

_____

_____

_____

Notes

_____

_____

_____

_____

_____

_____

_____

_____

_____

_____

_____

_____

_____

_____

Chapter 6

Grooming Basics

Alright, Let's Talk About Hair!

Hair is one of the most important parts of the body, for many reasons. It gives us a layer of protection and is one of the most noticeable aspects of someone. Regardless of whom that person may be, you will notice their hair or lack thereof. How your hair looks can greatly improve or diminish your overall outfit. By this point, you have heard me say that, or something similar, many times. First off, my apologies if it may bore you, but it is imperative that you understand that concept. Every aspect of how you present yourself will be judged by others, and more importantly, by yourself.

Now, let me move on to why it is important to keep your hair in check. First, it is important to take care of your hair; it will often be your centerpiece in many situations. I recommend building a habit that involves taking care of your hair. That way, it becomes natural, and you will be less likely to complain about doing it. Don't let sweat and oils build up for too long. That can lead to very messy and dirty hair. That's not to say that oil is bad for your hair. The body produces its own natural oils that provide many benefits to your hair. There is a three-day window when natural body oils soak into your hair. The third day has been seen to provide the many benefits to your hair, such as aiding in the repair of damaged cells, and providing a fuller body of hair. It is for this reason that I recommend not fully washing your hair every day. You can certainly rinse it, but I would only apply shampoo every three to four days. When you use shampoo, be sure to use conditioner. Shampoo strips the natural oils from your hair, so using conditioner afterward is recommended, as it can provide some of the nutrients the natural oils provided, back into your hair.

The second reason I recommend you keep your hair in check is that it simply looks much better. Unless you are replicating the *tousled* hairstyle, I recommend styling your hair into your preferred style. At the very least, comb your hair every day, as the act of combing your hair and scalp increases the flow of blood and nutrients to your hair, which keeps it healthy. Regardless of what style form you may be wearing, having a styled head of hair is great for simply looking awesome and feeling confident. One thing I have noticed is that, regardless of when I and many others get a haircut, an immediate feeling of confidence takes over. Whether you have just gotten a haircut or have re-styled your hair, there is a feeling of confidence that takes over, and it is a wonderful feeling. As I mentioned earlier in the book, when you are confident, people notice. You may find yourself smiling more, giving more compliments, or simply doing generous acts for others—the expressed confidence from within you impacts others. To think that all of that could come from simply keeping your hair in check.

Choosing Your Style

So, now that I have given you some basic grooming tips, it is time to talk about hairstyles. There are many different styles of haircuts one can receive. Certain styles are quite simpler than others, meaning that less experienced barbers can do them with ease. Others are far more complex and will require a more skilled and professional barber to complete. This is where the cost for a haircut can differ a fair bit. Some barber shops have flat rates, and others will factor in the complexity of the cut. Depending on what style you choose, be aware that you may have to pay a fair sum.

Let me move on to the styles you can choose. In my research to find the top hairstyles, I have consistently seen the following on nearly every list. There is no order to these; one is no better than the rest. They appear to be what is most commonly chosen. So, without further delay, let me list them off and give you a brief description of what they look like.

Bald: Although many wouldn't consider this a hairstyle, it is a form of manipulating hair. Bald is very self-explanatory; it consists of either a completely shaven head, or no hair on top, with only very short hair on the sides.

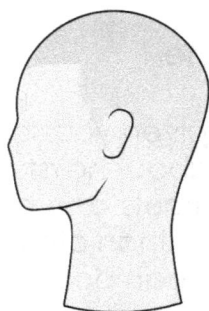

The Hockey Cut: The *hockey cut* is a style that consists of having long, wavy hair that is brushed back behind the head—not slicked back but pushed back, and styled to have some texture. Thick, long, and *voluminous* hair is needed for this style.

The Fade: The *fade* is a cut where the hair is cut very short along the sides of the head, and slowly increases in length until reaching the top of the head, where it is full length. Generally, the hair on top is still fairly short when compared to other styles.

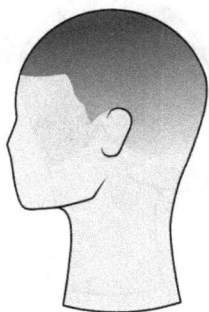

Tousled: The *tousled* style is meant to be much messier than any other style. The tousled style is when the hair is pushed back slightly and there is no further styling to be done—that is it. This is ideal for longer and thicker hair.

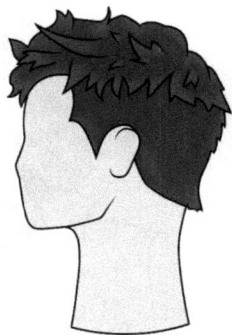

The Buzz Cut: The *buzz cut* is a very simple haircut, as it involves cutting the hair to a very short length. This is done all around the head to keep it uniform, and allows the hair to have minimal maintenance. A buzz cut should be no longer than roughly ¾".

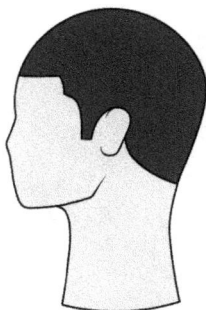

The Side Part: The *side part* is a style where the hair on the top of the head is combed neatly to the side; the hair on the sides is shortened but not faded, and there is a noticeable part in the hair. The part can be separated by combing the hair around it well enough, or by shaving the part to make it more permanent. This is often seen as being a classic business cut.

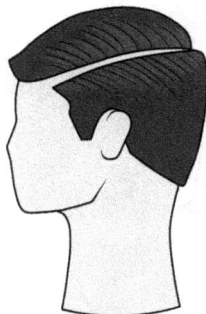

The Crew Cut: The *crew cut* is another low maintenance cut, and is very simple to manage. It consists of having the hair on the top of the head short (from 1 to 3 inches), and the hair on the sides of the head slightly shorter than that on the top. The hair on top should be a uniform length.

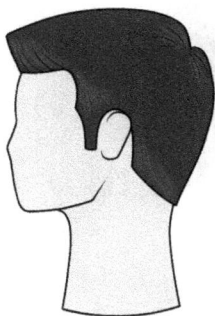

The Undercut: The *undercut* consists of having medium to long hair on the top, and shaved on the sides and back. The hair on top is generally brushed backward. This is another low maintenance cut.

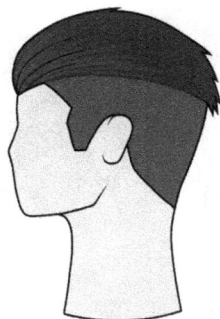

The Quiff: The *quiff* is an interesting cut. The hair on the sides of the head can be cut shorter or combed backward. The hair on top is brushed forward until it reaches the forehead, and that is when it is combed up and back. This creates much more volume around the front of the head. This can be a very demanding style, as it requires a fair amount of maintenance for it to look decent.

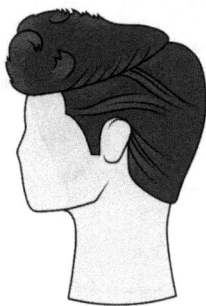

The Classic Pompadour: This hairstyle often looks similar to the quiff. The main difference between the two is that the pompadour will have a much smoother overall shape to it. But much like the quiff, it is a very demanding hairstyle, which requires time to be set aside in order to maintain it.

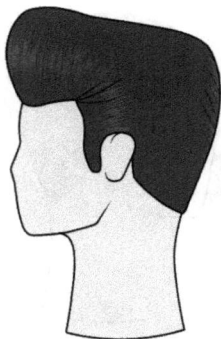

So, those are the main, generally most popular hairstyles I have found. It is important to note that these are what I consider the foundational cuts, meaning that many other styles often originate from these. If you have struggled to choose a hairstyle, I hope it helped. If you already have a preferred style, I hope this has given you a bit of insight into what else is available. I encourage you to experiment with different styles, and see what you prefer the most.

To Shave or Not to Shave

It is time to talk about facial hair, gentlemen. Should you grow it out or shave it off? The shaving/grooming industry is one of the largest in the world. This is because, whether we want to or not, we must manage our facial hair in some capacity. Facial hair is part of our genes, and so we all grow it when we pass through puberty. For some, the growth of facial hair will be rapid and will cover the face evenly. For others, it can be slow and uneven. This is why shaving is a huge part of men's lives. Most don't like the process, but regardless, unless you never touch your facial hair, shaving or grooming will be part of your life.

Beards are versatile for many reasons. They look great if properly taken care of, they can add another dimension to your general look and style, and they can protect you from the elements, depending on where you live. Beards have also been known to add an air of dominance and authority to those who bear them. When deciding to grow a beard, it is important to know that it will take some time to come in fully. You must be willing to endure the itchiness and unpleasant look of your beard for it to reach full maturity. To keep your beard healthy, I suggest creating a maintenance routine. You will want to trim any loose hairs, and use beard oils to keep it healthy and good looking. I will not tell you to use certain products, but I will encourage you to research and find products that you are comfortable using.

For those of you who prefer a clean-shaven face, having a shaven face can feel amazing, and helps to add a crisper look to your outfit. People with clean-shaven faces have also been noted to be more approachable and trustworthy. Now, for most of you, I am sure that shaving is a hassle. It takes away from your time, and it can hurt on occasion. As I mentioned, for beard maintenance, I recommend you make a routine based around shaving. Give yourself some time to enjoy the process, instead of just plowing right through. Taking longer allows one to see it as a craft, and to reduce possible injuries. Whether you have a routine or not, you must understand how to use your razor. It will be the tool that you use for this activity, so it is important to know what you use and what else you might consider using.

Cartridge Razors: The most common razors out there, and for good reason: they are convenient and do a very good job. The only problem I have noticed with cartridge razors is that they tend to cost a lot over a year. Cartridges wear out and need to be replaced, and they are not always cheap.

Safety Razors: More of a classic razor, these require some skill to use correctly; but they can offer a much closer shave than cartridge razors. Safety razors can be a bit more expensive as an initial purchase, but the cost to replace blades will be less than those of cartridge razors.

Straight Razors: A traditional razor that has been used for hundreds of years, these razors provide the cleanest shave but also require much skill to use accurately. These razors are generally inexpensive initially, and in the purchasing of new blades.

I recommend trying all of them to see what you prefer. Just note that you will need to practice with the safety and straight razors, to fully achieve a clean shave.

So, should you shave or not? That is completely up to you. If you can grow a beard, that might be the way to go. If you can get over the initial waiting period, you won't have to worry about fully shaving your face for a while. If you choose to shave, whether it's because you can't grow a beard or you prefer a clean face, I would continue down that path. That way, you don't have to worry if you have a good looking beard or not. In the end, it's all up to you. But please, regardless of which one you do, turn it into a routine. It will help you so much more.

"There should be a connection between a man's hairstyle and what matters to him in life."
– Barry Webster

Notes

_____

_____

_____

_____

_____

_____

_____

_____

_____

_____

_____

_____

_____

_____

Notes

_____

_____

_____

_____

_____

_____

_____

_____

_____

_____

_____

_____

_____

_____

_____

Chapter 7

Accessories

What Is an Accessory?

How could there be a book on style without including one of the most important aspects of one's wardrobe? Accessories are the little things that add a lot. If utilized correctly, accessories will add that extra personal touch to your look, and provide a bit of flare where there may not have been any. So, it might help to explain what an accessory is. An accessory is anything that can be removed from your person that will not drastically affect the look of the outfit. For example, if you are wearing a suit that fits and looks good, and then you decide to remove your tie clip, It will not affect the overall look of the outfit too much. However, you will notice that the tie clip is gone, and you will potentially feel that the outfit is missing something. This is because accessories bring another dimension into your wardrobe. They add that little bit extra to your overall presentation. To help you get a better idea of what accessories are, let me list a few.

The **tie clip**, as previously mentioned, is quite self-explanatory; it is a clip that holds the midpoint of your tie to your shirt, and prevents it from hanging if you were to lean over or move quickly.

A **watch** is a classic, and probably the one accessory most people know of. Watches are used to keep track of time by the busy working man.

A **pocket square** is another classic piece of menswear. It is slipped into the breast pocket of the suit. It provides both a wonderful addition of color to the outfit, as well as acting as a handkerchief if needed.

Cufflinks are another great accessory, especially if you want to dress more formally. They are a decorative piece that is meant to fasten both sides of a shirt cuff.

These accessories will likely be the ones you will see the most, as they are easy to incorporate into most outfits. The cufflinks and pocket square are the only ones that would require a more formal outfit for best results.

How They Can Improve Your Look

So, how can you use accessories to raise your outfit to another level? First off, you need to know what style form you will be, or are currently dressed in. If you are wearing an outfit in the casual spectrum, accessories such as cufflinks and pocket squares, as I mentioned, will not raise your outfit to a higher level as much as they could if paired with a more formal outfit. To me, a watch is the best all-around accessory, regardless of what style you choose to wear. This is because it offers the most visual impact and has a functional purpose.

It is important to note that not all watches will amplify your outfit. Having a watch that is oversized, cheaply made, or even more childlike, will not help you improve the visuals of your outfit. On the other hand, having a watch that looks great but is not functional, for whatever reason, can be a hindrance. I cannot bring myself to wear a watch if it is not functional; however, to each their own.

Now that we have the more pessimistic view out of the way, let me talk about the little details that can make accessories amplify your outfit even more than you thought. When buying a watch, or any accessory for that matter, keep in mind two very important things: Does the metal match any metal you may be wearing, or does the leather match any leather you may be wearing? If you are confused by that, don't worry; I was as well when I first ran into this concept. In short, do your best to match metals and leathers. This means, if you are wearing a brown leather belt, do your best to wear a watch that has a brown leather band that is as close in color as you can. The same can be said with metals. If the buckle on your belt is silver, do your best to use a watch that is primarily silver. It is even better if your watch and belt match completely. This little detail of matching can raise your outfit to a whole new level. People who are not as fashion conscious will see that you look more put together than normal; they will not fully understand how they know, as it will be picked up by their subconscious. Those who have a deeper understanding of fashion will notice the little details and will think more positively of you for including them.

There are so many accessories out there for you to try out. If something takes your fancy, try it out, and incorporate it into your outfit if you can. Just be sure not to have an accessory that is far too flashy, as it can be far too distracting. Keep your accessories simple and reliable to begin with; then branch out into more exotic designs as your confidence grows. Accessories are available for you to have fun and improve your look, so don't be scared to pay a pretty penny for them. I will be going over why you should spend for quality, in the next chapter.

"When you feel that you look good, you will feel good, and then you will look good."
– Curtis Banks

Notes

_____

_____

_____

_____

_____

_____

_____

_____

_____

_____

_____

_____

_____

_____

Notes

_____

_____

_____

_____

_____

_____

_____

_____

_____

_____

_____

_____

_____

_____

Exercise:

Notes

_____

_____

_____

_____

_____

_____

_____

_____

_____

_____

_____

_____

_____

_____

Chapter 8

Quality Over Quantity

What Counts as Quality?

I'm sure you have heard this saying before: "Quality over quantity." Well, it's a saying that has lasted a very long time, for a reason. It tells the truth. If you were to invest in a quality pair of shoes, or a dress shirt—or hell, even a pair of socks—they would last you so much longer than the cheaper version. Would you rather buy one excellent pair of dress shoes, and have them as part of your wardrobe for years, or would you prefer to buy an average, off-the- shelf pair, and replace them every year? The answer should be **obvious**. Now, that is all well and good, but it might help to have an understanding of what makes something *good quality*. As I have already mentioned dress shoes, let's keep them as our primary example of how to spot quality.

Shoes are generally constructed in one of three ways.

Bonded:
When the upper part of the shoe (that which is over your foot) is glued to the sole of the shoe (the bottom half of the shoe), with an adhesive.

Blake Stitched:
When the upper half of the shoe is stitched to the sole of the shoe.

Goodyear Welted:
When the upper and sole are connected, not by stitching directly together, but instead by having a welt that connects to both individually. To clarify, the welt is stitched to the upper in one location, and then the welt is stitched to the sole in a different location. The upper and sole are not directly stitched together.

A good quality pair of dress shoes will be either blake stitched or goodyear welted. Bonded shoes are very unlikely to last as long. The adhesive will wear out over time, and the shoe will slowly separate. A good quality pair should be able to be resoled a few times if need be. The sole of the shoe will wear out over time, regardless, but depending on which type of construction the shoe was made of, the shoe can be resoled multiple times. Every time a bonded shoe is separated and resoled, the upper gets damaged, and will only last a hand full of resoles before it just won't work anymore. When a blake stitched shoe gets resoled, the stitching will be along the same upper strip. This can lead to the holes widening and the upper breaking down, to the point where the entire shoe will need replacing. This will last far longer than a bonded shoe. Finally, a goodyear welted shoe can have the sole replaced many times, as the only part that would need replacing is the welt. It will not suffer from the same wear and tear like the other two would.

Now, that is just one aspect of what to look for in a shoe. Just that alone is a fair bit of information you may want to take into consideration. The quality of the leather will also be one to think about. This is not just applicable to shoes; anything you buy, you will want to check for its quality. If you are buying a shirt, checking the thread count or seeing if there are any loose threads would be a good idea. Regardless of what it may be, do a quick check. The best way to determine the quality would be to research the item you are looking at. See if there is a list describing how it was made, look at customer reviews of the product, or ask someone at the shop to see if they can help you out. Finding that out is essential.

Why It Can Save You Money in the Long Term

With all of that in mind, what would be the financial benefit of buying a quality item? When you buy a high-quality item, you know that it will look good and last a long time. Lasting a long time is the part of any quality item that will end up saving you money later on. Although the upfront cost of the item will be significantly higher than most, the long-term saving of it when compared to cheaper items will be very apparent. As I briefly mentioned previously, it is better to buy one quality pair of dress shoes that will last you a long time, than to buy a new pair every year or two. The cost of purchasing a new pair every so often will quickly equal the cost of the quality pair you could have gotten, and will only become more expensive as time goes by.

It is important to note that quality items will need upkeep and maintenance occasionally. You will be hard pressed to find someone who throws out quality items just because they require cleaning or general maintenance. Yes, this process will have an associated cost to it but is still financially and professionally more sound than replacing the item.

As I previously mentioned, some of these items can wear out and will need fixing. Going back to the example of dress shoes or boots that require a sole replacement, once that process is completed, and assuming that the shoe is still in very good condition, it can be resold. There are always people looking for quality boots or shoes at a cheaper than normal price. If you happen to have a pair that you no longer need, or can't wear for whatever reason, you can sell them to make back some money.

The biggest reason is, of course, because you won't need to buy more and more clothes or accessories constantly. Now, this may not seem viable, and it may not be viable for many of you at this moment, but if you can, invest in one thing of high quality. It will be scary to many of you, but the long-term payoff is huge. You have to be willing to do it.

The Attitude of Wealth

I feel it necessary to briefly talk about the attitude of wealth while on the topic of quality. The essential fact about anything that is of a good or higher quality is that it will cost more than a simple, off-the-shelf item— sometimes far more than you may think. Now, the brand associated with the item will factor into the price, but I am not here to talk about clothing brands. The only thing that should matter is the quality of the item. The reason I wish to talk about the attitude of wealth is that for many of you, there will always be the urge to stick with something cheaper. I can understand where that comes from. I was in a position where my income was very low for quite some time. However, I knew the path I wanted to head down, so I committed to invest in a pair of boots that were quite pricey. I have them to this day and use them often. They have done me very well.

If you are reading this, it shows that you want to dress better in some way, for a certain reason. The reason does not matter, but if this is what you truly want to do, you have to change your perceptions about money. Now, I will not go into detail, because this is a book on style, after all. To go through this process, it will cost you, and you have to acknowledge that. If you struggle financially set up a system where a small portion of your income is put toward high-quality items. Even if it allows you to get only one item every few months, go for it. It is better to have a system in place; that way, you know what you have available to you.

Once you get to the point where you are looking great and are confident in yourself, you will likely find that more opportunities come to you. I mentioned this in a previous chapter. Just have confidence in yourself, and change your perception of money. If you find this hard to get into, I understand; do your best with what is available to you. If that is the case, this next section might give you some hope.

There Are Exceptions

There are exceptions to the rule. Yes, you read that correctly. There are indeed exceptions. There are not many exceptions to the rule, but they do exist: certain items that are inexpensive and are of good quality. I have found that these items mainly come from companies that are purposely making inexpensive items so more people can use them. Other places I have been pleasantly surprised by are certain wholesale stores, or direct from the manufacturer. These places can be a little harder to find or purchase from, because they usually rely on bulk orders as their main form of distribution. In some instances, I have found great products in discount stores. If you want to explore these options, the best way of doing it would be to look it up or ask around. Surprisingly, most people do want to help you out, contrary to what you may think. Ask around on social media, and I'm sure you will find something.

Another exception might be to wait for the item you're interested in to go on sale. In my opinion, if there is a sale on something that you like, and you are sure it is of high quality, go for it. You will not find exceptions often, but if you do, leverage it.

There is not much more I can say regarding this. Exceptions to the rule are always available; it just might take more time and effort to find them. If you want to dress up the best you can, but you are on a budget, visit a discount store. If there is one rule that I recommend sticking to, it is this: If you believe something is an exception to the rule, and it is an article of clothing, try it on. That way, you can have a better sense of its true quality. If you find something online, make sure it is from a reputable source. If you follow that rule, you should be set.

"The best things in life are free. The second best are very expensive."
–Coco Chanel

Notes

_____

_____

_____

_____

_____

_____

_____

_____

_____

_____

_____

_____

_____

_____

Notes

_____

_____

_____

_____

_____

_____

_____

_____

_____

_____

_____

_____

_____

Chapter 9

Find Your Style

Everyone's Style Is Unique

As the chapter name indicates, this section of the book will be going over how to find your style. It is so important to find your style as it allows you to create whatever image of yourself you want. This greatly impacts your brand, for better or for worse. As you are reading this book, it is more likely that you want to better your brand. For a quick recap, your brand is what others will think of you when they see you or hear your name. You want this to be positive: The better the brand you have, the more people will trust you.

If you take some time to observe people, you will find that everyone has a unique style. Some may not recognize this fact, but everyone has or does something that makes them unique. It could be something as simple as someone wearing their watch on the right arm instead of the left, or that they always have a spare set of dress clothes set aside just in case they need it. You need to find what makes you unique. If it can help you stand out in a good way, keep it. If not, get it gone. The best thing I can recommend you do while undertaking this style initiative is to create something that makes you unique. Start from scratch, and rebuild what makes you unique.

Many things can make you unique. It can be an article of clothing you wear or even a mannerism. Whatever it may be, make sure you are confident wearing or doing it. Make sure that it does not offend others. This can be a difficult one to deal with because, regardless of what you do or wear, someone will likely take offense to it, and many won't tell you that they are offended. This has more to do with how you act, so do your best not to come off as snobby or smug. It may take you some time to find something you are happy with and that others acknowledge and don't take offense to. (Don't forget, it's your life.)

What Experimenting Involves and Why You Should Do It

The point of finding something unique is to help you make your style. As you know, there are many different styles to choose from. I call these the foundational styles. From these, other styles can be made. This is where experimenting comes into play. To find your style, you must first choose which foundational style you want to emulate the most. Let's say, for this example, that you want to emulate a more casual style. So, the first step is done; you have chosen the foundational style.

The next step is to choose an aspect of the style you would like to remove or add something to. You love the general look of Casual, but you want to add a little bit of formality to it. That completes the second step, choosing to add or remove.

The third step is to identify what item, in particular, you want to focus on. In this example, we know that this person wants to add a little bit of formality to the overall outfit. After identifying what he wants to change, he chooses the shoes. He wants to remove the sneakers, as they are very casual, and he wants to add something with more formality in their place. That completes step three.

Step four is to choose what footwear (in this case) he will use in their stead. He decides to go with a pair of leather boots. Knowing that boots are more formal and are still functional for everyday use, he incorporates them into his outfit.

In that example, we had someone choose their favored foundational style, identify what aspect of it they wished to change, and then had them choose something to replace it. By choosing to add a more formal item, the entire outfit was moved more toward Smart Casual. Just by adding one item, the outfit is now between two of the foundational styles. This instantly causes the outfit to be more unique and personal.

This is why experimenting is so important. It allows you to blend the foundational styles in order to help achieve your style. The more you experiment, the better you become. The better you become, the more unique you become. After some time, you will know exactly what you like and what you don't. With that knowledge, you can truly put an outfit together and say, "This is my style."

This process will take time, and you will probably go through a few phases along the way. Don't worry about it; enjoy the experience as it is happening. I will take an educated guess and say that you will probably learn more and get a deeper under-standing of style and fashion by experimenting. All of the books on style and fashion are great and can teach you a lot, but they still don't compare to the hands-on experience.

Adapting Your Style for Different Events/ Functions, and When to Respect the Guidelines

Adapting your style for an event/function that has a dress code is something you will learn over time. It ties directly into your experience of experimenting and how well you know your style. Many events all over the world have required dress codes. Some events allow all style forms as long as they are not sloppy; some events want Business dress, and some only allow you in if you wear Black Tie. Depending on what the dress code is and how strictly it is enforced, you will need to take into consideration how you can adhere to the code, while also incorporating your unique touch.

A great example would be a black tie event. If you are someone who likes to come off as the more creative type, and your uniqueness comes from your creative look, you must find a way to fit it into Black Tie. Luckily for you, that problem can easily be solved. Creative Black Tie is an offshoot of the foundational Black Tie. With Creative Black Tie, you can add more color to your outfit. Be sure not to overdo it by adding too much color. Although it is Creative Black Tie, it is still Black Tie. On the plus side, Black Tie and Business dress are the only style forms that will restrict what you normally would incorporate into your outfits. You should be fine with any other event dress code.

So, what if you are not going to an event? What if you need to adapt your style to your place of work? Well, that will all depend on where you work. If you work in more of an office environment, you can probably wear your style without too much worry. If, however, you work in a more rugged environment (for example, in a warehouse or around machinery), I would recommend your clothing choices be more on the side of functionality than anything else. In these environments, safety should be the priority, and your style and uniqueness should be secondary. For this, you want to follow the guidelines.

Following the guidelines is another aspect to adapting your style in certain events or situations. As I just mentioned, following the guidelines can factor into your safety, depending on what you may be doing. If, however, you are working in a more conservative workplace, or attending a very strict Black Tie event, you may be seen as less respectful if you do incorporate your style and uniqueness into it. My recommendation—as long as you know that you can get away with adding your personal touch during a more formal event or workplace, without offending the culture—is to go for it. If you are not sure if it will be accepted, stick with the designated dress code, and don't deviate from it.

"Fashion you can buy, but style you possess. The key to style is learning who you are, which takes years. There's no how-to road map to style. It's about self-expression and, above all, attitude."
– Iris Apfel

Notes

_____

_____

_____

_____

_____

_____

_____

_____

_____

_____

_____

_____

_____

Notes

_____

_____

_____

_____

_____

_____

_____

_____

_____

_____

_____

_____

_____

Notes

_____

_____

_____

_____

_____

_____

_____

_____

_____

_____

_____

_____

_____

_____

_____

Chapter 10

Have Fun and Be Confident

Alright, gentlemen! This final chapter will focus on how to have fun and be confident with your outfit/outfits of choice. You have come this far and have gained the knowledge to put yourself together in a way that is unique to you. It may take a while for you to gain complete confidence while wearing an outfit, especially if it is more outside of your comfort zone than normal. If you feel that applies to you, here is what I can recommend to help you gain confidence.

Wear the Outfit – Build Confidence by Dressing Your Style Whenever You Can

Yes, that does seem ridiculous, but it works. Wear the outfit whenever and wherever you can. Doing this will increase your confidence by making it a habit. When people are in the process of a habit, it means that (for the most part) they are in an unconscious state. They have done such a thing so many times that they no longer need to think about it. It becomes a habit. The same can be said when getting used to an outfit. The best way to increase your confidence while wearing it is to make it a habit. When you make it a habit, you won't think about it. You won't have to worry about how confident you feel while putting it on.

This is not to say that you will never feel confident while wearing your outfit. You will, once you turn the act of putting it on into a habit. After you are wearing the outfit, then you can look in a mirror and see who you have become. The first thing you will likely feel is confidence in yourself just for wearing the outfit. Although you may have put it on while in an unconscious state, the second you look at yourself, you become conscious of the fact that you are wearing it.

As I stated earlier, the best way to start this process is to wear the outfit whenever and wherever you can. The best thing I can recommend is to wear it around your house or place of living. Even if no one is there to see you, put it on. It will become a habit, and that will lead to confidence. If you want to gain confidence at a faster pace, push your comfort zone. Wear your outfit to events, or even when meeting up with friends you haven't seen in a while. These are great because you will also have to listen to any criticism you may get from others. There are always positive and negative sides to criticism; if you get some positive criticism, see how you may use it to better your overall outfit. If you receive some negative criticism, let it go, and continue to wear your outfit as you intended. Being faced with these situations, while you are still gaining confidence in your outfit, will help immensely when this outfit becomes your go-to.

Once you realize that you are no longer worried about other people's opinions, and have complete confidence with yourself, that is the moment to have fun. Look into the mirror and realize that you have completely changed your perception of yourself. This is a monumental achievement because you can now truly own your style. It is now your *perfect personal style*. No one can take that away from you now.

Notes

Notes

Notes

Recap of Main Points

Now that we are nearing the end of the book, let us quickly go over what we have learned thus far.

There are eight foundational **style forms**:

Sloppy/Untidy
Ultra-Casual
Casual
Smart Casual
Business Casual
Business
Black Tie
White Tie

Each of these styles is comprised of certain types of clothes that would be considered more or less formal. Each style will inform others of who you are, based on which style you wear. Examples include people thinking much less of you if you were to wear the Sloppy style of clothing, and people thinking much more positive things toward you when wearing Smart Casual or Business.

2) The **style pyramid** is an essential piece of knowledge if you wish to eventually master your style. Knowing the pyramid—fit, fabric, and function—and how they impact every article of clothing you wear or buy, will allow you to make smarter choices if purchasing an item or just going somewhere you haven't gone before. A question you will find yourself asking is, "What would be the function of this?" The most important aspect of style, regardless of what you may be buying, is *fit*. Fit is king and will do the most good for you. It is better to have a cheap casual outfit that fits well, than to have a $7000 suit that does not fit.

3) In this chapter, we discussed the **basics of clothing items**, including the difference between the types of pants and what you might use them for. We also discussed which foundational style form certain clothes would be in, and why, as well as what can be put together to create a great outfit.

4) In regard to **leveraging colors**, in this chapter, we learned why adding color is the key to looking great, and how colors can add to the outfit to make it more personal. We learned what colors generally work best for most people, and how you can use them. Finally, we learned what some of the colors represent, and people's perceptions of them.

5) In this chapter, we outlined the most common forms of **footwear**—sneakers, dress shoes, boots, etc.—what the benefits are to each type of shoe, what they represent, and lastly, the formality of the shoe: what it is that makes it more or less formal.

6) In this chapter, we learned the **basics of grooming**, what it entails, and why it is important to manage your hair and keep it clean and tidy. We discussed choosing a hairstyle that works for you, and we went over the most popular hairstyles. Finally, there was a quick discussion on whether or not to grow/keep a beard or to shave, and what tools you could use.

7) The **basics of accessories** were discussed in this chapter. We discussed what an accessory is, what counts as an accessory, and why they are imperative to leveling up your outfit, as well as how this can be done.

8) In this chapter, we talked about **what counts as quality**, why it can save you money in the long term, the attitude of wealth, and the few exceptions to the rule.

9) In chapter nine, we discussed how to **find your style** and how everyone has a unique style. We talked about how to experiment, what it involves, and why you need to experiment in order to find your style, as well as how to adapt your style to certain situations or events, and when to follow the guidelines of them.

So, these have been the topics discussed in the book. I am very glad that you have made it this far. I truly hope you apply what you have read, and use it to create your own *perfect personal style.* Thank you so much for reading the book. If you need anything, head over to DressingUpNow.com to get more information, as well as larger, higher quality images of what was seen throughout the book.

With that, I wish you the best of luck in your style journey. Take care.

Sincerely

Scott Smythe

"Style is the only thing you can't buy. It's not in a shopping bag, a label, or a price tag. It's something reflected from our soul to the outside world— an emotion."
– Alber Elbaz

Notes

_____

_____

_____

_____

_____

_____

_____

_____

_____

_____

_____

_____

_____

_____

Notes

_____

_____

_____

_____

_____

_____

_____

_____

_____

_____

_____

_____

_____

_____

Notes

_____

_____

_____

_____

_____

_____

_____

_____

_____

_____

_____

_____

_____

Glossary

Accessories: *An article or set of articles of dress, such as gloves, earrings, or a scarf, that adds completeness, convenience, attractiveness, etc. to one's basic outfit.*

Accommodating: *Easy to deal with; eager to help or please; obliging.*

Acknowledge: *To admit to be real or true; recognize the existence, truth, or fact of.*

Adaptability: *Able to adjust oneself readily to different conditions.*

Adhesive: *A substance that causes something to adhere, as glue or rubber cement.*

Analyze: *To examine carefully and in detail so as to identify causes, key factors, possible results, etc.*

Appropriate: *Suitable or fitting for a particular purpose, person, occasion, etc.*

Articles: *An individual object, member, or portion of a class; an item or particular.*

Aspects: *A way in which a thing may be viewed or regarded; interpretation; view.*

Associated: *To connect or bring into relation, as thought, feeling, memory, etc.*

Attitude: *Manner, disposition, feeling, position, etc., with regard to a person or thing; tendency or orientation, especially of the mind.*

Beneficial: *Conferring benefit; advantageous; helpful.*

Birthday Suit: *To be completely naked (as people are at birth)*

Circumstances: *A condition, detail, part, or attribute, with respect to time, place, manner, agent, etc., that accompanies, determines, or modifies a fact or event; a modifying or influencing factor.*

Combinations/Combined: *To bring into or join in a close union or whole; unite.*

Comedian: *A professional entertainer who amuses by relating anecdotes, acting out comical situations, engaging in humorous repartee, etc.*

Complement: *A thing that completes or brings to perfection.*

Condition: *A particular mode of being of a person or thing; existing state; situation with respect to circumstances.*

Confidence: *Belief in oneself and one's powers or abilities; self-confidence; self-reliance; assurance.*

Conservative: *Disposed to preserve existing conditions, institutions, etc., or to restore traditional ones, and to limit change.*

Contrary: *Opposite in nature or character; diametrically or mutually opposed.*

Convenient: *Suitable or agreeable to the needs or purpose; well-suited with respect to facility or ease in use; favorable, easy, or comfortable for use.*

Demonstration: *The act or circumstance of proving or being proved conclusively, as by reasoning or a show of evidence.*

Designates: *To nominate or select for a duty, office, purpose, etc.; appoint; assign.*

Deviate: *To depart or swerve, as from a procedure, course of action, or acceptable norm.*

Differing: *To be unlike, dissimilar, or distinct in nature or qualities.*

Diminished: *To make or cause to seem smaller, less, less important, etc.; lessen; reduce.*

Discernible/Discern: *To perceive by the sight or some other sense or by the intellect; see, recognize, or comprehend.*

Discount: *To offer for sale or sell at a reduced price.*

Dominance: *Psychology – the disposition of an individual to assert control in dealing with others.*

Drastically: *Extremely severe or extensive.*

Durability: *Able to resist wear, decay, etc.; well lasting; enduring.*

Elegant: *Gracefully refined and dignified, as in tastes, habits, or literary style.*

Emulate: *To try to equal or excel; imitate with effort to equal or surpass.*

Environment: *The aggregate of surrounding things, conditions, or influences; surroundings.*

Essential: *Absolutely necessary; indispensable.*

Exotic: *Strikingly unusual or strange in effect or appearance.*

Expectation: *The act or state of looking forward or anticipating.*

Experimenting: *A test, trial, or tentative procedure; an act or operation for the purpose of discovering something unknown, or of testing a principle, supposition, etc.*

Flexibility: *Susceptible of modification or adaptation; adaptable.*

Gala: *A festive occasion; celebration; special entertainment.*

Generous: *Liberal in giving or sharing; unselfish.*

Habitual: *Commonly used, followed, observed, etc., as by a particular person; customary.*

Hardy: *Capable of enduring fatigue, hardship, exposure, etc.; sturdy; strong.*

Hierarchy: *Any system of persons or things ranked one above another.*

Immensely: *Vast; huge; very great.*

Impression: *The first and immediate effect of an experience or perception upon the mind; sensation.*

Inappropriate: *Not appropriate; not proper or suitable.*

Individual: *A distinct, indivisible entity; a single thing, being, instance, or item.*

Inherently: *Existing in someone or something as a permanent and inseparable element, quality, or attribute; inhering.*

Intertwined: *An act of twining, twisting, or interweaving.*

Intricate: *Complex; complicated; hard to understand, work, or make.*

Judgment: *The ability to judge, make a decision, or form an opinion objectively, authoritatively, and wisely, especially in matters affecting action; good sense; discretion.*

Knowledge: *Acquaintance with facts, truths, or principles, as from study or investigation; general erudition. Familiarity or conversance, as with a particular subject or branch of learning.*

Leveraged: *Power or ability to act or to influence people, events, decisions, etc.; sway.*

Liberal: *Favoring or permitting freedom of action, especially with respect to matters of personal belief or expression.*

Maintenance: *Care or upkeep, as of machinery or property.*

Mannerism: *A habitual or characteristic manner, mode, or way of doing something; distinctive quality or style, as in behavior or speech.*

Monumental: *Exceptionally great, as in quantity, quality, extent, or degree.*

Occasion: *A special or important time, event, ceremony, celebration, etc.*

Offended: *To irritate, annoy, or anger; cause resentful displeasure in.*

Oxblood: *A deep, dull-red color.*

Perceived: *To recognize, discern, envision, or understand.*

Perception: *Immediate or intuitive recognition or appreciation, as of moral, psychological, or aesthetic qualities; insight; intuition; discernment.*

Perspective: *The state of one's ideas, the facts known to one, etc., in having a meaningful interrelationship.*

Pessimistic: *Pertaining to or characterized by pessimism or the tendency to expect only bad outcomes; gloomy; joyless; unhopeful.*

Profound: *Of deep meaning; of great and broadly inclusive significance.*

Puberty: *The period or age at which a person is first capable of sexual reproduction of offspring: in common law, presumed to be 14 years in the male and 12 years in the female.*

Pyramid: *A quadrilateral masonry mass having smooth, steeply sloping sides meeting at an apex; a* system or structure resembling a pyramid, as in hierarchical form.

Quality: *High grade; superiority; excellence.*

Quantity: *A considerable or great amount.*

Regardless: *Without concern as to advice, warning, hardship, etc.; anyway.*

Resoled: *To put a new sole on (a shoe, boot, etc.).*

Routine: *Commonplace tasks, chores, or duties as must be done regularly or at specified intervals; typical or everyday activity.*

Rugged: *Having a roughly broken, rocky, hilly, or jagged surface.*

Solution: *A particular instance or method of solving; an explanation or answer.*

Spectrum: *A broad range of varied but related ideas or objects, the individual features of which tend to overlap so as to form a continuous series or sequence.*

Subconsciously: *Existing or operating in the mind beneath or beyond consciousness.*

Synthetic: *Noting or pertaining to compounds formed through a chemical process by human agency, as opposed to those of natural origin.*

Glossary

Tousled: *Disordered or disheveled.*

Traditional: *In accordance with tradition.*

Unique: *Existing as the only one or as the sole example; single; solitary in type or characteristics.*

Urge: *To push or force along; impel with force or vigor.*

Vamp: *The portion of a shoe or boot upper that covers the instep and toes.*

Variations: *The act, process, or accident of varying in condition, character, or degree.*

Versatile: *Capable of or adapted for turning easily from one to another of various tasks, fields of endeavor, etc.*

Wardrobe: *A stock of clothes or costumes, as of a person or of a theatrical company.*

About the Author

Scott Smythe was born in Surry, England, in 1999. He moved to Canada at a very young age and has spent his life growing up in Ottawa, Canada.

The author will continue to find new ways of helping men find, create, and own their style. His primary focus is to turn this book, and future books, into an online webinar series, where anyone can receive a more detailed and visual representation of his expertise. For any questions or information regarding this project or book, please contact the author directly, at Confidence@dressingupnow.com.

To order more books, please visit www.Amazon.com.

If this book has made an impact on you and how you dress, please let others know of what you have learned. It is so important to give back to others and help them along their journey. This world needs and deserves people who look their best and are confident with themselves. So please, go out and make a difference.

www.ingramcontent.com/pod-product-compliance
Lightning Source LLC
Chambersburg PA
CBHW070405200326
41518CB00011B/2078